dad jokes

every

25-year-old

dad

should

know

Copyright © 2020 by Ben Radcliff

All rights reserved. No part of this publication may be reproduced, distributed, or transmitted in any form or by any means, including photocopying, recording, or other electronic or mechanical methods, without the prior written permission of the publisher, except in the case of brief quotations embodied in critical reviews and certain other noncommercial uses permitted by copyright law.

Introduction

Just because you're a 25-year-old dad doesn't mean you shouldn't be improving your dad jokes game.

This excellent book of dad jokes is, at the same time, both pretty punny and pretty awful. Now you can be a perfect pain in the neck at the next family gathering or party when you spring these bad dad jokes on everyone.

But why wait until then? These great one-liners and wordplay jokes are perfect for the dinner table, a long car ride with kids, business meetings, toasts, or when you want to impress (or not impress) the people around you.

Read these jokes straight through, skip around, or play the **Try Not To Laugh Dad Jokes** game on the next page.

Every good dad knows – bad dad jokes are just how you and eye roll!

Try Not To Laugh Game Rules

Easy Version

1. Find an opponent or split up into two teams.
2. Team 1 reads a joke to Team 2 from anywhere in the book.
3. The person reading the joke looks right at the opposing person or team and can use silly voices and funny faces if they wish.
4. If Team 2:

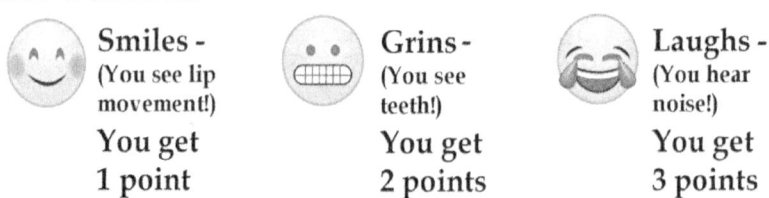

Smiles - (You see lip movement!)	Grins - (You see teeth!)	Laughs - (You hear noise!)
You get 1 point	You get 2 points	You get 3 points

5. Read one joke at at time, then switch the giving and receiving teams.
6. The team with most points after five rounds wins! Use the score sheets on the following pages.

Challenge Version

1. Same rules apply except you get one point if you can make the other team laugh. No points for smiling or grinning.

Good luck and try not to laugh!

SCORE SHEET

	TEAM 1	TEAM 2
ROUND 1		
ROUND 2		
ROUND 3		
ROUND 4		
ROUND 5		
TOTAL		

	TEAM 1	TEAM 2
ROUND 1		
ROUND 2		
ROUND 3		
ROUND 4		
ROUND 5		
TOTAL		

	TEAM 1	TEAM 2
ROUND 1		
ROUND 2		
ROUND 3		
ROUND 4		
ROUND 5		
TOTAL		

	TEAM 1	TEAM 2
ROUND 1		
ROUND 2		
ROUND 3		
ROUND 4		
ROUND 5		
TOTAL		

	TEAM 1	TEAM 2
ROUND 1		
ROUND 2		
ROUND 3		
ROUND 4		
ROUND 5		
TOTAL		

	TEAM 1	TEAM 2
ROUND 1		
ROUND 2		
ROUND 3		
ROUND 4		
ROUND 5		
TOTAL		

	TEAM 1	TEAM 2
ROUND 1		
ROUND 2		
ROUND 3		
ROUND 4		
ROUND 5		
TOTAL		

	TEAM 1	TEAM 2
ROUND 1		
ROUND 2		
ROUND 3		
ROUND 4		
ROUND 5		
TOTAL		

SCORE SHEET

	TEAM 1	TEAM 2
ROUND 1		
ROUND 2		
ROUND 3		
ROUND 4		
ROUND 5		
TOTAL		

	TEAM 1	TEAM 2
ROUND 1		
ROUND 2		
ROUND 3		
ROUND 4		
ROUND 5		
TOTAL		

	TEAM 1	TEAM 2
ROUND 1		
ROUND 2		
ROUND 3		
ROUND 4		
ROUND 5		
TOTAL		

	TEAM 1	TEAM 2
ROUND 1		
ROUND 2		
ROUND 3		
ROUND 4		
ROUND 5		
TOTAL		

	TEAM 1	TEAM 2
ROUND 1		
ROUND 2		
ROUND 3		
ROUND 4		
ROUND 5		
TOTAL		

	TEAM 1	TEAM 2
ROUND 1		
ROUND 2		
ROUND 3		
ROUND 4		
ROUND 5		
TOTAL		

	TEAM 1	TEAM 2
ROUND 1		
ROUND 2		
ROUND 3		
ROUND 4		
ROUND 5		
TOTAL		

	TEAM 1	TEAM 2
ROUND 1		
ROUND 2		
ROUND 3		
ROUND 4		
ROUND 5		
TOTAL		

I looked longingly into my wife's eyes and whispered, A.E.I.O.U and sometimes Y.
Best wedding vowels ever.

An usher in a theater notices a man sprawled across three seats. "I'm sorry, sir, but you're allowed only one seat," the usher says. The man just lies there, so the usher asks, "What's your name?"
"Sam," the man replies.
"Where'd you come from, Sam?"
"The balcony."

What do you do when balloons are hurt?
You helium.

My coworker called me selfish for reheating salmon in the microwave.
"But it's not shellfish!" I replied.

The robbers took everything from my house, but I'm most upset they took my mirror.
I can't see myself without it.

Before I die I am going to eat a whole bag of unpopped popcorn.
That should make the cremation a little more interesting.

What's a shark's favorite game?
Swallow the leader.

My wife just accused me of having zero empathy.
I don't understand how she can feel that way.

What kind of street does a ghost like best?
A dead end.

I've got a friend who reminds me of a software update.
Every time I see him I groan, "Not now."

What kind of fire leaves a room damp?
A humidifier.

What's a cannibal's favorite snack?
A knuckle sandwich.

What did the waitress say to the man who wouldn't stop staring at her while she was refilling his glass?
"Take a pitcher, it'll last longer!"

If fruit comes from a fruit tree, what kind of a tree does a chicken come from?
A poul-tree.

What kind of hat does a soda pop wear?
Bottle cap.

Did you know that Davy Crockett had three ears?
A right ear, a left ear and a wild frontier.

I got caught stealing a leg of lamb from the supermarket.
The security guard yelled, "What are you doing with that?"
I replied, *"Hopefully braise it with potatoes and some gravy would be nice as well."*

What do you call a group of Whales on a TV show?
A podcast.

Do not spell the word "part" backward.
It's a "trap".

Son: Dad, did you get a haircut?
Dad: **No, I got them all cut.**

What are terminators called when they retire?
Exterminators.

You should sing solo.
So low I can't hear you.

Dad: I need to call the doctor today.
Mom: Which doctor?
Dad: **No, the regular kind.**

I've been told I'm condescending.
That means I talk down to people.

What do you call a baby monkey?
A chimp off the old block.

I've been sending my herbs in the mail.
I wanted to know if thyme travel was possible.

Where does someone who is really vague live?
Vegas.

My dad's sister works in a Paris bakery and hates it.
She's a cross aunt.

What's a cow's favorite painting?
The Moona Lisa.

There is a new restaurant named Karma.
It doesn't have a menu.
You just get what you deserve.

At first I thought it was great marrying an archeologist.
But then I found out she was a gold digger and my life is in ruins.

What animal should you never play hide-and-seek with?
A Peking duck.

How did the soup lose its job?
It got canned.

Did you hear about the man who gave his chimps to the zoo?
They came with a monkey-back guarantee.

Just saw a man slumped over his lawnmower, bawling his eyes out.
He said he'll be fine; he's just going through a rough patch.

I just burned 2,000 calories.
That's the last time I leave brownies in the oven while I nap.

Music is coming out of the printer.
I think it's jamming again.

Having a cellphone makes it really easy to cheat on my wife.
My son sometimes stands behind her and texts me what cards she has in her hand.

What do you call a mouse that swears?
A cursor.

A termite walks into a bar and asks,
"Is the bar tender here?"

How do you make a bandstand?
Take away their chairs.

I recently decided to sell
my vacuum cleaner.
All it was doing was gathering dust.

My grandmother was famous all over town for growing delicious strawberries. She made me promise that when she died, I would plant her strawberries on her grave so that people could enjoy them when they visited. When she passed away I fulfilled my promise. **She's dead and berried.**

I thought my neighbors were nice people. **Then they went and put a password on their wi-fi.**

Change is inevitable, except from a vending machine.

A man was found guilty of overusing commas.
The judge warned him to expect a really long sentence.

"Officer, are you crying while you are writing me a ticket?"
Officer: **It's a moving violation.**

Who is bigger, Mr. Bigger or Mr. Bigger's baby?
Mr Bigger's baby, because he's a little Bigger.

What happened after the man
ate a dozen donuts?
He developed a glazed look on his face.

An old lady was knitting as she drove.
A police officer drove up alongside
her and yelled, "Pull over!"
The lady yelled back, **"No, they're mittens."**

How many tickles does it take to make an
octopus laugh?
Tentacles.

We all know Albert Einstein was a genius.
But his brother Frank was a monster.

My friend is getting rich by taking pictures of salmon dressed in human clothes.
It's like shooting fish in apparel.

Just been reading a new book all about a short ballerina.
"The Girl with the Dragging Tutu."

What did the sofa say when it got hurt?
"Couch!"

A man showed up for a duel armed only with a pencil and paper.
He then proceeded to draw his weapon.

Give a man a fish and you will feed him for the day.
Teach a man to fish and he's going to spend a fortune on gear he'll only use twice a year.

Dad: See? To prove I'm not a boring dad I went and got a tattoo!
Daughter: Oh, cool! It's.. uh?
Dad: (proudly) It's a picture of a thermos!
Daughter: Well, uh, the detail is certainly...
Me: **Hey, don't touch the thermos tat.**

What should you increase to get to the airport faster?
Terminal velocity.

Did you hear about the guy who was in the water but said he wasn't?
He was in the Nile.

I hate how funerals are always at 9:00 or 10:00 AM.
I'm really not a mourning person.

What do you call bears with no ears?
B.

Did the pasta do it?
Gnocchi didn't.

A man was caught stealing from a supermarket today while balanced on the shoulders of two vampires.
He was charged with shoplifting on two counts.

A pirate walks into a bar with a paper towel on his head. The bartender says, "What's with the paper towel? "
The pirate says, **"Arrr... I've got a bounty on me head."**

Which cards are the best dancers?
The king and queen of clubs.

Anyone want to help me make a TV show about Abraham Lincoln?
The plan is to shoot it in front of a live audience.

When I was ten my mom told me to take my brother to a movie so she could set up for his surprise birthday party.
It was then I realized he was her favorite twin, not me.

Why did dad get angry when the window was broken?
Because it was a pane to replace.

My son was recently rehearsing for a play, and he kept falling through the trapdoor. We took him to the doctor, who said not to worry, **it was just a stage he was going through.**

Converting the number 51, 6 and 500 to Roman numerals doesn't just make me mad, **it makes me LIVID.**

Cashier: Would you like your milk in a bag?
Dad: **No, just leave it in the carton.**

My friend David lost his ID.
Now I call him Dav.

I've done some terrible things for money.
Like getting up early to go to work.

What do "Game of Thrones" and "The Sixth Sense" have in common?
Icy dead people.

What do you call a dog with no legs?
You can call him whatever you like, he's never going to come.

I don't like to brag about how all my friends let me borrow their brass instruments.
I just don't feel like tooting my own horn.

What do you call a guy with kids in Holland?
An Amsterdad.

Where do you imprison a skeleton?
In a rib cage.

My friend is obsessed with taking blurry pictures of himself while taking a shower.
He has serious selfie steam issues.

God finally answered my prayers for winning the $50 million lottery.
The answer was, "No".

BREAKING NEWS!
Police are currently investigating a raid at Tiffany's in London.
The suspects were last seen running just as fast as they can.

My friends laughed at me when I said I had a hot date and they said she was imaginary.
Well the last laughs on them because they're imaginary too.

Why aren't koalas considered bears?
They don't have the correct koalafications.

Sometimes I talk to myself when I'm alone and it's kind of sad.
"Me too."

What color is the wind?
Blew.

Did you hear about the Spanish train robber?
He had loco motives!

Why do Mafia guys always have the cleanest cars?
From all the whacks.

What do you call a chicken crossing the road?
Poultry in motion.

What do you call a fear of giants?
Fee-Fi-Phobia.

I went to a haunted bed and breakfast in France.
The place was giving me the crepes.

A nice cop left a note on my windshield to let me know I'd parked my car correctly.
It said PARKING FINE.

How do pigs talk to each other?
Swine language.

I just found out I'm colorblind.
The diagnosis came out of the purple.

What do you call a sad cup of coffee?
Depresso.

If you run in front of a car you get tired; if you run behind a car you get exhausted.

What is a prisoner's favorite punctuation mark?
The period. It marks the end of a sentence.

What do you call a horse that lives next door?
A neigh-bor.

I didn't eat anything other than brown bread for dinner.
That was my wholemeal.

The day I found my first grey hairs,
I thought I'd dye!

Why did the iPhone go to the dentist?
He had a blue tooth.

What do you call it when animals with long cylindrical tube-like bodies and no limbs take over the world?
Global worming.

Why couldn't the Avon lady can't talk?
Because her lipstick.

What is the difference between unlawful and illegal?
One is against the law, the other is a sick bird.

Studies show cows produce more milk when the farmer talks to them.
It's a case of in one ear and out the udder.

I blame Mother Earth for all earthquakes.
It's her fault.

What do you call a bird that flies into a fan?
Shredded tweet.

I've just opened an Elvis Presley themed steak house.
It's aimed at people who love meat tender.

What would you say if you had breakfast with the Pope?
"Eggs, Benedict?"

What did Jay-z call his wife before they got married?
Feyoncé.

Wife: Stop being an idiot, just be yourself.
Dad: **Make up your mind.**

I couldn't understand why my dog was motionless.
Then I realized, it was on paws.

Did you hear about the guy who got fired from the calendar factory?
He took a day off.

What's white, furry, and shaped like a tooth?
A molar bear.

I used to play the triangle in
a Jamaican reggae band.
*I decided to leave because it was
just one ting after another.*

How do you know when you're caught in
freezing rain?
It hurts like hail.

Judge: Why should you be released early?
Man: I'm.
Judge: Go on.
Man: I think.
Judge: Yes?
Man: Can I please finish my sentence?
Judge: **Sure. Parole denied.**

What do you call a man who's been dead 10,000 years?
Pete.

I didn't think I was fat until the McDonald's worker said, **"Sorry about your weight."**

I was so bored that I memorized six pages of a dictionary.
I learned Next to Nothing.

What should you do if there are 14 frogs on your car's back window?
Use your rear window de-frogger.

My wife refuses to go karaoking with me
so I have to duet alone!

I saw a man going up a hill with a trolley full of horseshoes, four leaf clovers and rabbit's feet.
I thought, **"Well he's pushing his luck!"**

What did the doctor say to the patient suffering from a bacterial infection?
"Ah, I see you're a man of culture as well."

How do you upset a dinosaur?
Touchasaurus Spot.

Why is a Panda the most dangerous animal in the animal kingdom?
Because it eats shoots and leaves.

Why are curious people so good at singing?
Because they inquire.

I used to be in a band called Missing Cat.
You probably saw our posters.

Just got a birthday card, opened it and rice went everywhere!!
It was from Uncle Ben!

I have a lot of jokes about unemployed people.
But none of them work.

What's the relationship between people buying pizza and people selling it?
They both want each other's dough.

Why did the dinosaur newspaper shut down?
Ratings were killed off by social meteor.

What do you call someone who delivers Indian food?
A currier.

I just started a business building boats in my attic.
Sails are going through the roof.

What's a Jedi's favorite candy?
A Lifesaver.

What did one earthquake say to the other?
"Hey, it's not my fault!"

The police just knocked at my house to tell me my dog was chasing a kid on a bike.
I just closed the door because my dog doesn't even have a bike.

My dad died when we couldn't remember his blood type.
As he died, he kept insisting for us to be positive, but it's hard without him.

The origami boxing match was showing the other night.
Shame though as it was only on paper-view.

I got a universal remote for my birthday.
This changes everything.

A blind man walks into a bar...
and a chair, a table, and some people.

What do you call a German who is going bald?
Herr Loss.

Dad: Doctor, I feel like a pony.
Doctor: *Don't worry, you're just a little hoarse.*

You know the problem with grapes these days?
People just aren't raisin them right.

Do leprechauns make good secretaries?
Sure, they're great at shorthand.

What do you call a smelly sheep?
A P-ewe.

What do you call a vegetable that helps direct a film?
A producer!

What type of rock is never delivered on time?
Slate.

Why did St. Patrick drive all the snakes out of Ireland?
He couldn't afford plane fare.

Is it crazy how saying sentences backwards creates backwards sentences saying how crazy it is?

I went to IKEA yesterday.
It was a Swede experience.

Just read a book about Stockholm syndrome.
It started off badly but by the end I really liked it.

A man leaves home, takes three left turns, then is confronted by two masked men. Who are they?
The umpire and the catcher.

Hummingbirds are just regular birds that can't remember the lyrics.

You know you have a severe iron deficiency
when your shirt is all wrinkled.

I told the doctor I felt like
a deck of playing cards.
He said he'd deal with me later.

What happened to the man who went to a
seafood disco?
He pulled a mussel.

Why was Humpty Dumpty
optimistic for winter?
Because he had a great fall.

Did you hear about the cat who swallowed a ball of yarn?
She had a litter of mittens.

Turning vegan would be a big missed steak!

My friend's bakery burned down last night.
Now his business is toast.

Tried changing my password to "14days" but it was two week.

Our local bird sanctuary has been closed due to one of the birds having a sinus infection.
I think it's the phlegmingo.

I got fired from my lawn maintenance job.
I was just not cutting it.

Patient: I'm afraid of the vertical Axis.
Therapist: Why ?
Patient: **Yes!**

I recently ate at a restaurant where they charge you for bad manners.
I guess that's what you call fine dining!

In 2020 I'm thinking of starting up a new business, recycling discarded chewing gum.
I just need some help getting it off the ground.

Son: Dad, use the word "dispose" in a sentence.
Dad: *Please hold dispose while I I get my camera.*

Two atoms are walking along.
One of them says:
Oh, no, I think I lost an electron.
Are you sure?
Yes, I'm positive.

You hear about the latest book on poltergeists?
It's flying off the shelves.

I told my son that I wash my hair with poo but I lied.
It's not real poo, it's sham poo.

What do you call a chickpea that walks off a cliff?
Falafell.

I bet no one will see this one coming.

1.

What exactly is an acorn?
Well in a nutshell, it's an oak tree.

Why was the pizzeria so slow?
The servers were down.

Why did the woodpecker go to the gym?
So he could have nice pecks.

I ordered a takeout from the local Chinese restaurant last night. I ordered a 23, a 13, a 31 and a 79. I had to take them back.
They all tasted odd.

I asked a real estate agent how much it would cost to buy a hockey stadium.
But she said she could only give me a ballpark estimate.

My best friend called me and said, "An evil wizard turned me into a tiny harp! I don't know what to do!"
I went to his house to find out he's a little lyre.

My wife has been leaving jewelry catalogs all over the house.
So, I've taken the hint and got her a magazine rack for her birthday.

I can always tell when someone is lying just by looking at them.
I can tell when they're standing too.

What's an angle's favorite dip?
Slantro.

What do you call a Satanist who only eats low-carb pizza?
The anti-crust.

As I suspected someone's been adding soil to my garden.
The plot thickens!

What do you call a nervous javelin thrower at a Renaissance fair?
Shakespeare.

My grandfather tried to warn them about the Titanic.
He screamed and shouted about the iceberg and how the ship was going to sink, but **all they did was throw him out of the theater.**

What fish goes up the river at 100mph?
A motor pike.

Be careful what you do in college.
Bad things you will follow you, fraternity.

I've just burned my Hawaiian pizza.
I should have put it on aloha temperature.

Do you know why ancient Egyptians had such a hard time getting workers?
Their pyramid scheme.

What is blue and doesn't weigh much?
Light blue.

How many cops does it take to screw in a light bulb?
None. It turned itself in.

I never make mistakes.
I thought I did once, but I was wrong.

Me and my brother inherited some furniture from the local zoo.
My brother was angry because I got the lion's chair.

A guy walks into the bank, pulls out a gun, points it at the teller and screams, "Give me all your money or you're geography!"
The teller says, "Don't you mean history?"
The robber replies, *"Don't change the subject!"*

Son: Dad, I'm hungry.
Dad: *Hi hungry, I'm Dad...*

I really hate elevators.
I'm going to start taking steps to avoid them.

What do you call an alligator in a vest?
An investigator.

He who does a Good Turn daily, must get dizzy after a while.

Did you know I used to have a job crushing cans?
It was soda pressing.

Three guys are on a boat with four cigarettes but nothing to light them.
So they throw one cigarette overboard and the boat becomes a cigarette lighter.

My pregnant wife asked me if I was worried the temperature inside her would be too hot for the baby.
I said, "Nope. It's womb temperature."

I recently took up meditation.
It's better than sitting around doing nothing.

Why did the capacitor kiss the diode?
He just couldn't resistor.

My friend Jay had twin girls recently and he wanted to name them after him.
So I suggested Kaye and Elle.

And the Lord said unto John, "Come forth and you will receive eternal life."
John came in fifth but still won a toaster.

Hung a picture up on the wall the other day.
Nailed it.

Why did the scientist go to the tanning salon?
Because he was a paleontologist.

Waiter: How do you like your steak, sir?
Sir: Like winning an argument with my wife.
Waiter: **Rare it is.**

What do snowmen do in their spare time?
They chill.

What do you get if you cross a centipede and a parrot?
A walkie talkie.

My son swallowed some coins
and was taken to a hospital.
When I asked how he was the nurse said,
"No change yet!"

If April showers bring May flowers, what do May flowers bring?
Pilgrims.

How much does it cost to buy a big boat?
A yacht.

I don't always tell dad jokes.
But when I do he always laughs!

Printed in Great Britain
by Amazon